Chakras

A Coloring Book by

Paul Heussenstamm

Pomegranate

PORTLAND, OREGON

Pomegranate Communications, Inc.
19018 NE Portal Way, Portland OR 97230
800 227 1428   www.pomegranate.com

Pomegranate Europe Ltd.
'number three', Siskin Drive, Middlemarch Business Park
Coventry CV3 4FJ, UK
+44 (0)24 7621 4461   sales@pomegranate.com

Pomegranate's mission is to invigorate, illuminate, and inspire through art.

Front cover:
Paul Heussenstamm (American, b. 1949)
Chakraman Blue
Oil and acrylic on canvas, 101.6 x 76.2 cm (40 x 30 in.)

Back cover: First Chakra, Chakra Grouping, Chakra Parts, Seventh Chakra

Item No. CBK010

Cover design by Patrice Morris

Printed in China

26 25 24 23 22 21 20 19 18 17   10 9 8 7 6 5 4 3 2 1

CHAKRAS

A note from the artist

THANK YOU for allowing me to share with you my knowledge of the chakra system, or the vital energy centers of your subtle body. Chakras are important in maintaining good health, strengthening your immune system, and expanding your capacity to be fully alive. For the past thirty years, I've been exploring, feeling, seeing, and painting the body's energy patterns and learning to understand their intrinsic value. The essence of chakra awareness goes back to ancient times in India and Tibet, to the beginnings of meditation, yoga, and early disciplines of consciousness. The word *chakra* means a wheel or circle of energies found within the spinal column and the body. The universal or standard chakra system consists of seven major chakras that start at the base of the spine and move up to the top of the head.

Included here are simple sketches of each chakra. The chakra system is a perfect rainbow starting with red at the base of the spine moving up to pure white at the crown of the head.

- The first chakra (red), located at the base of the spine, is known as the root chakra (*muladhara* in Sanskrit). Its intrinsic capacity is for survival, security, foundation, patience, and fluidity. This base chakra is how we are connected with the earth.
- The second chakra (orange) is found just below the navel and is considered the sacral chakra (*swadhishthana*). Its function is sexuality, connectivity, fantasy, and sensuality. It is associated with water and how we are sensitive to feeling.
- The third chakra (yellow) is just below the heart and is known as the solar plexus. Here we find our power source, color, fame, authority, karma, and passion. This chakra is where we have our chi (our vital energy or "fire") and our courage.
- The fourth chakra (green) is located at the heart and is better known as the heart chakra (*anahata*). The attributes of the heart chakra are unconditional love, affinity, compassion, and healing presence, and it is associated with air. It is how we relate to life and the world.

+ The fifth chakra (blue) is known as the throat chakra (*vihuddha*). It is the chakra of artists, poets, and singers, and is associated with unity, knowledge, resonances, manifestation, and imagination. It is how we are able to create and to interact with a creative universe.

+ The sixth chakra (purple or indigo) is known as the brow chakra or third eye. The "third eye" is the center of intuition, clairvoyance, self-realization, and authenticity. This chakra is where we see into the higher consciousness and where we experience the spiritual teachings of our existence.

+ The seventh chakra (pure white) is considered the crown chakra (*shasrara*). It is located at the crown of the head. This energy of higher consciousness is the energy of illumination, divine truth, consciousness, and union with the universe. The seventh chakra points to where we connect with the gods, goddesses, and spirits, and where we experience or witness our religious beliefs.

+ + +

The drawings in this book are a foundation to discovery and awareness of chakras and the energy systems of the body. Understanding the seven chakras, also referred to as the seven levels of energy or consciousness, can free us from a lack of energy, ease our fears, and bring joy, beauty, and health to our daily lives.

While coloring each chakra template in this book, it is important to slow down, focus, and enjoy the act of coloring. Choose whichever colors feel right, as it is truly a meditative practice you're about to explore. In the chakra tradition, engaging by coloring increases the movement of your chakra energies. Once the chakra energy opens, your prana (life breath) increases, which leads to heightened awareness and the possibility of expanded health. Our chakras have been active since we were born, whether we are aware of their energy or not. Knowledge about this system can be beneficial to balance your well-being. I encourage you to simply let go; just color and let the mind dream, and awaken when the drawing is finished!

Hand-Drawn Chakra Imagery

1. Chakra Energy
2. First Chakra
3. Ancient Chakraman
4. Chakra Parts
5. Advanced Heart
6. Fourth Chakra Eyes
7. Meditation
8. Chakra Tree
9. Chakra Spiral Mandala
10. Chakra Balance
11. Cosmos Chakraman
12. Chakra Direction
13. Chakra Dance
14. Chakra Living
15. Chakra Elements
16. Chakra Moon
17. Chakra Even
18. Seeing Eyes
19. Chakra Octagon
20. Chakra Grouping
21. Chakra Chevron
22. Chakra Ganesh
23. Chakra Lines
24. Sixth Chakra Swirls
25. Chakra Symbols Mandala
26. Chakra Woman
27. Seventh Chakra
28. Chakra Roots
29. Chakra Rounds
30. Chakra Shield
31. Chakra Stance
32. Chakra Time
33. Chakra Tree of Light
34. Chakra Turns
35. Chakra Vibrations
36. Chakra Master
37. Continuum
38. Balance
39. Creative
40. Endless Chakra
41. Chakra Man
42. Lower Chakra
43. Open Heart
44. Sun Man
45. Sixth Chakra Open
46. As Above So Below
47. Symbols
48. Sacred Symbols
49. Chakra Mind
50. Wheel

1

4

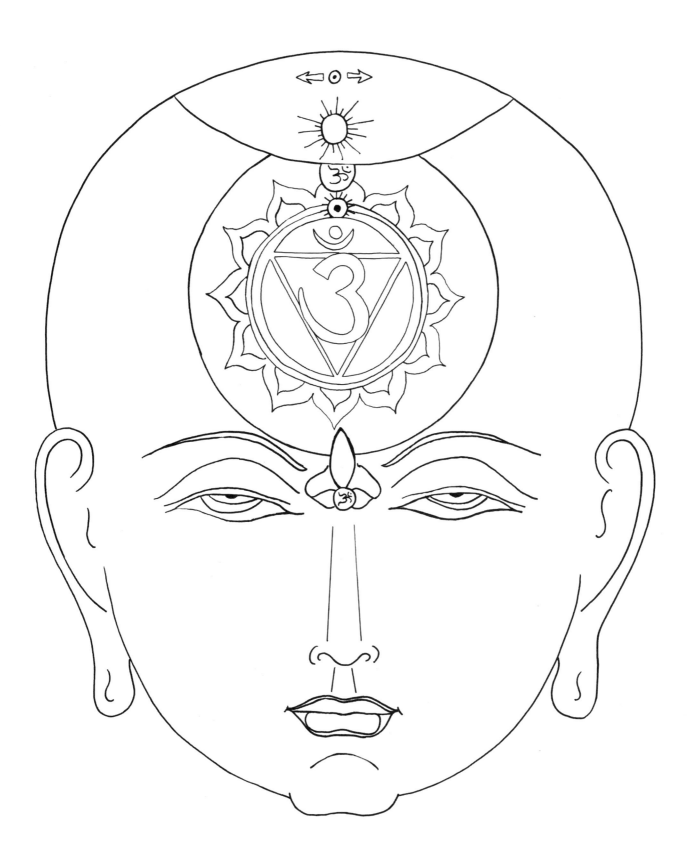

8

9

15

19

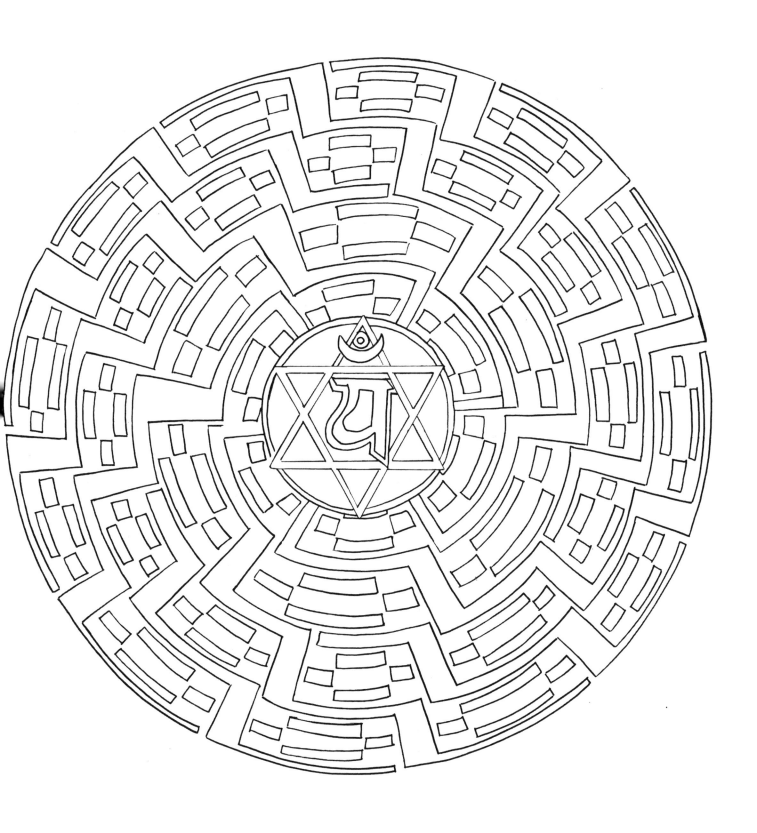

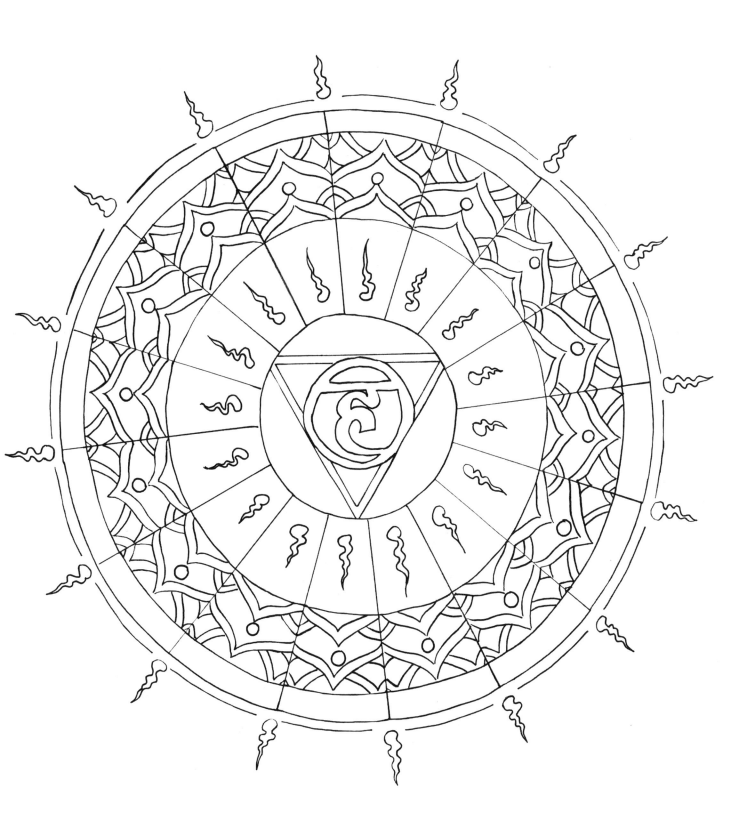

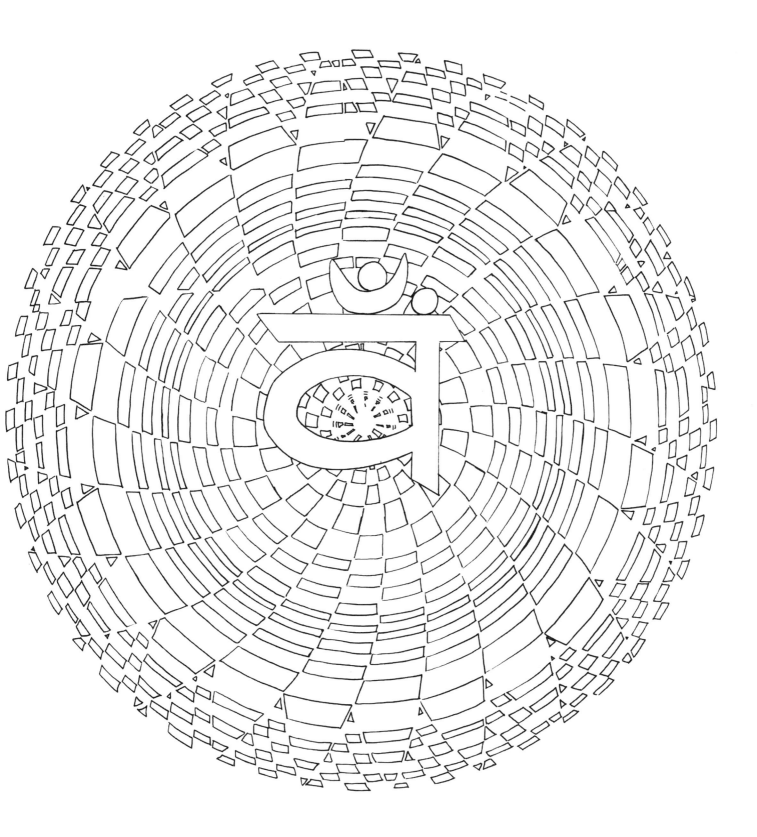

37

43

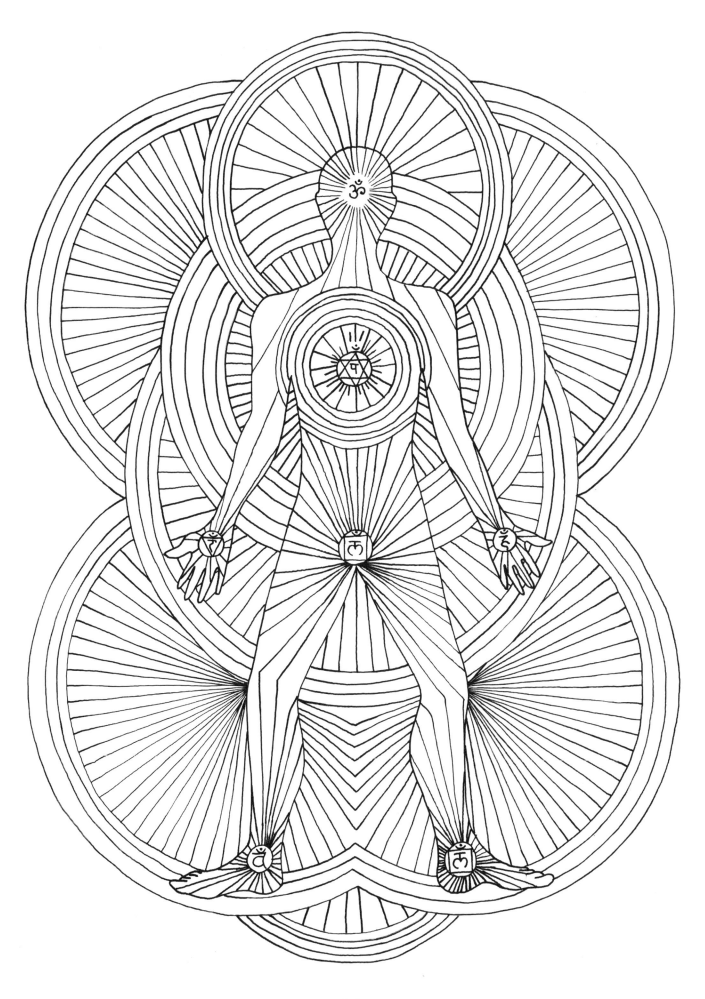

44

48

50

houghtfully conceived
and engagingly intricate,
Pomegranate's coloring
books combine stunning illustrations,
high-quality paper, and sturdy
construction to delight generations
of coloring enthusiasts. With
subjects ranging from fine art,
nature, and architecture to history,
the metaphysical, and more,
Pomegranate's coloring books
offer something for everyone.
Visit www.pomegranate.com
to see our full selection.